The Song of Humanity: From Stones to Silicon

Mantra Bhatt

BookLeaf Publishing

India | USA | UK

Presentation by *BookLeaf Publishing*

Web: www.bookleafpub.com

E-mail: info@bookleafpub.com

ISBN: 9789363315563

First edition 2024

DEDICATION

To my mother, my rock, Komal

To my dad, my hero, Niraj

To my best friends, who have been by my side since childhood.

To my fur siblings, Apollo and Goldie, bundles of Joy

PREFACE

Humanity, the most intriguing journey the world has ever seen. I still remember the day I first read the *Mahabharata* when I was a wee kid. Even though I was never a believer, a part of my mind kept pondering over it. As a 5-year-old, I was fascinated by the romanticized portrayal of war on such a large scale. However, as I grew older, my perspective on it changed. I began to view the characters as mere humans and delved upon the intricacies of their nature, the conflicted personalities, and the horrors of war that absolutely devastate civilization. There began my journey of analysing and pondering on the conflicts and peculiarities of human nature throughout human history. Soon after, I started putting my thoughts into words, which was, until quite recently, only in prose. Finally, I tried my hand at poetry during the COVID-19 pandemic and absolutely loved it. I realized I wanted to write on topics that aren't as commonly explored in poetry, such as war, death, betrayal, success, failure, and disease, to name a few. The story of humanity is by far the most intriguing one ever because the way we moved from defenseless apes to the masters of the world is simply awe-inspiring and in some ways, shocking and humbling.

Through this book, I would like you, the reader, to accompany me on a journey through the song of humanity. Together, we will explore the conflicting nature of humankind, the turmoil of so-called Great Men, the rise and fall of civilizations and the events that shaped us into who we are today.

Happy reading, fellow human.

INDEX

Out of Africa

In the dawn of time, on ancient earth so wild,
Our prehistoric ancestors roamed the land,
Two-legged beings, curious and beguiled,
Exploring realms untouched by human hand.

They journeyed far across the vast expanse,
Through forests dense and mountains towering
high,
Enduring hardships, facing danger's dance,
Their spirit bold, their courage soaring nigh.

From Africa's savannahs they did emerge,
A noble tribe of hunters forged in flame,
Their senses keen, their instincts on the verge,
Surviving in a world they could not tame.

They crossed the seas on rafts of woven reeds,
Seeking new horizons, distant shores,
Adapting to the land's compelling needs,
Learning ancient wisdom from the earth's core.

Through icy tundra and steaming jungle heat,
They trudged along in search of sustenance,
Their journey fraught with challenges elite,
Their fate determined by their perseverance.

In caves they sought refuge from the storm,
Huddled close to fires that flickered bright,
Their stories etched in paintings bold and warm,
A testament to their enduring plight.

And so they roamed the earth, a primal band,
Exploring realms beyond their wildest dreams,
Their legacy a tale of strength and grand,
A journey etched in time, in nature's schemes.

Though millennia have passed, their spirit lives,
In every step we take upon this earth,
Their journey echoes in the wind that gives,
A voice to those who dared to seek their worth.

The Dawn of the Ancients

In a time long forgotten, before the rise of
empires grand,
There existed ancient civilizations, born from
fertile lands.
From the banks of great rivers to the peaks of
towering mountains,
The first societies emerged, ushering in a new
era of foundations.

In Mesopotamia, the cradle of civilization,
Sumerians thrived,
Mastering the arts of writing, mathematics, and
law, they survived.
Ziggurats soared towards the heavens, temples
dedicated to the divine,
Their legacy etched in cuneiform tablets, a
testament to their design.

In Egypt, the Nile's life-giving waters nurtured a
majestic realm,
The pharaohs ruled with god-like power, their
tombs a lasting helm.
Hieroglyphs adorned temples and pyramids,
symbols of their glory,

They worshipped Ra, the sun god, in a
never-ending story.

The Indus Valley bloomed with cities of planned
precision,
Harappans traded goods and ideas, a culture of
inclusion.
Their cities laid out in grids, with advanced
drainage systems of clay,
Innovation and prosperity marked their way.

To the west, in ancient Greece, city-states
flourished with pride,
Intellectual pursuits and democracy, their
citizens' guide.
From the wisdom of philosophers to the bravery
of warriors bold,
Their legacy endures, a beacon of stories untold.

In the Americas, Mayans built towering
pyramids in the sky,
Incan empires stretched across vast landscapes,
reaching high.
Aztecs worshipped gods of sun and war, their
empire vast and strong,
Their achievements in agriculture and
astronomy, a legacy long.

The first civilizations, though gone, live on in
our memory,
Their contributions to human history, an
enduring legacy.
From the fertile crescent to the Andes' lofty
peaks,
Their stories echo through time, the dawn of the
ancients we seek.

Builders of Eternity

In the shadow of the mighty Sphinx's gaze
I toil beneath the scorching desert sun
A laborer among thousands in a haze
Of sweat and dust until the day is done

With bare hands and backs bent low, we build
The pyramids that pierce the clear blue sky
Their silent stones with secrets still concealed
In every block we lift, in every sigh

I wonder as I stack each heavy stone
What purpose does this monument serve?
Why are we slaves to build a tomb of bone
For a pharaoh's glory, never to preserve?

The hot wind whispers secrets in my ear
Of ancient gods and spirits long gone by
I feel their presence near, and sense their fear
As though they watch us with their ancient eye

We build with blood and tears and sweat
Our bodies broken by relentless toil
Yet still we work, our minds in deep regret
For our lives lost in service to the royal soil

I dream of freedom in the dead of night
Of escaping this eternal tomb's embrace
Of wandering far beyond the desert's blight
To find a home in some faraway place

But still I rise with the coming dawn
To face another day of endless tasks
To work until my weary limbs are drawn
To their breaking point, to complete what the
pharaoh asks

The pyramid grows taller with each passing day
Its stone blocks reaching for the heavens high
A monument to a king who fades away
While we, the laborers, are left to die

But in my heart, a flame of defiance burns
A spark of hope that will not be extinguished
I will not rest until the pharaoh learns
That we are more than slaves, we are
distinguished

For in the sweat of our brow and the strength of
our hands
We build a legacy that will not fade
Our names may be lost in drifting sands
But our spirits will linger in the shade

So let the pharaoh gaze upon his tomb

And know that we, the laborers, were not weak
For in our hearts a fire will always bloom
A flame that no darkness can ever seek

And when the pyramids stand
For centuries to come in the desert's glow
Know that we, the laborers, built this land
With our thoughts and dreams, in the sun's warm
glow.

The Hot Gates

In ancient days of Greece, when gods and heroes
roamed,
There lived a fearless warrior, whose legend has
been honed,
His name was Leonidas, king of Sparta bold,
Whose bravery and valor, in tales have been
told.

At Thermopylae's narrow pass, the Persian army
came,
Led by Xerxes, their mighty king, with soldiers
all aflame,
Their numbers seemed unstoppable, their swords
and shields a gleam,
But Leonidas and his Spartans stood firm, like a
mountain stream.

Three hundred men of Sparta, with hearts as
strong as steel,
Marched to face the Persians, determined not to
yield,
They knew the odds were against them, but still
they did not fear,
For in their veins ran warrior blood, and their
courage was sincere.

For days they fought like lions, against the
Persian horde,
Their swords flashed in the sunlight, their battle
cries a chord,
They held the pass at Thermopylae, against all
odds and more,
Their bravery and sacrifice, forever to adore.

Leonidas, the fearless king, with his sword and
shield in hand,
Fought at the front lines, leading his Spartan
band,
He inspired his men with courage, with a spirit
fierce and bold,
And in their hearts, his words of valor forever
told.

But as the days passed by, the Persians began to
press,
And despite their valiant efforts, the Spartans
could not suppress,
The overwhelming numbers of their foe, who
seemed to never tire,
Yet still they fought on bravely, their hearts
filled with fire.

In the end, the Spartan warriors fell, one by one
they died,

Their bodies littered the pass, a testament to
their pride,
But their sacrifice was not in vain, for their
deeds would never fade,
In the annals of history, forever they would be
displayed.

Leonidas, the brave and true king, fought to his
dying breath,
His legacy of courage, in the face of certain
death,
Would live on through the ages, as a symbol of
the free,
A Spartan king at Thermopylae, who fought for
liberty.

So raise a toast to Leonidas, with a hearty
Spartan cheer,
For his memory lives on, in the hearts of all who
hear,
Of his legendary deeds at Thermopylae, where
he made his stand,
A true hero of Greece, the pride of the land

Amicicide

In ancient days of Macedon's might,
A tale of honor lost and rage took flight.
The great King Alexander, young and bold,
Feared by some and loved by others told,
Of a tragic event that tore apart,
The bonds of friendship, once held close in
heart.

In the midst of celebration grand and gay,
With wine and joy to chase the night away,
Cleitus, a trusted friend and warrior true,
Chose to speak words that made the king
eschew.
He dared to question Alexander's fame,
And call into doubt the glory of his name.

A heated argument did soon ignite,
As tempers flared in the flickering light.
The king, incensed, his wrath did rise,
And in a moment of madness surprised,
He seized a spear, a weapon swift and sharp,
And plunged it deep into Cleitus' heart.

The room fell silent at the dreadful deed,
As blood spilled forth, a river black and freed.

The king, aghast at what his hand had done,
Cursed the gods for this fate, the battle won.
But victory tasted bitter in his mouth,
For friendship lost was payment from the south.

The aftermath of this tragic strife,
Cast shadows long o'er Alexander's life.
Guilt and sorrow weighed upon his soul,
As rumors spread of his heart turned cold.
He mourned the loss of his loyal friend,
And prayed for solace that would never end.

The people whispered of the king's cruel act,
And questioned if his rule was based on fact.
But Alexander, burdened by his shame,
Sought to make amends and clear his name.
He honored Cleitus with a grand tomb,
And built a shrine to banish all the gloom.

But peace eluded the troubled king,
For ghosts of the past would forever cling.
The memory of that fateful night,
Haunted his dreams, a never-ending fight.
And though he conquered lands far and wide,
In his heart, Cleitus' death could never hide.

So let this tale of Alexander be told,
Of a friendship shattered by anger bold.
A cautionary fable, a lesson learned,

That even kings can be caught and burned.
For pride and power, when taken too far,
Can lead to a kingdom left scarred and marred.

Kalinga

In the wake of Kalinga's bloody fight,
The emperor stood on fields of red,
His heart weighed down by sorrow's blight,
A kingdom conquered, but a soul not fed.

For Ashoka's thoughts were filled with dread,
As he gazed upon the countless dead,
The warlust that had once consumed his mind,
Now left him feeling lost and blind.

The cries of widows pierced his ears,
The wails of orphans filled his heart,
The stench of death, his soul it sears,
As he vowed to make a brand new start.

No longer would his kingdom bleed,
He'd sow the seeds of peace and heed.

He raised his eyes up to the sky,
And begged the heavens for a sign,
A way to mend the damage done,
And bring his people back to shine.

Through meditation, he found his way,
In Buddha's words, he saw the light,

A path of non-violence he'd convey,
To conquer hate with love, not fight.

He built great pillars across the land,
Inscribed with edicts of his new decree,
To spread compassion and understand,
To heal the wounds of history.

His thoughts now turned to legacy,
To build a kingdom based on peace,
To rule with wisdom, not tyranny,
And make all wars and hatred cease.

For Ashoka knew the cost of war,
The toll it took on human souls,
And vowed to spread peace near and far,
To make his kingdom truly whole.

And so the emperor's reign was marked,
By acts of kindness, not fear,
His thoughts of Kalinga still stark,
But now replaced with hope sincere.

His legacy would live on strong,
In tales of kindness and of grace,
For Ashoka's thoughts, they did belong,
To peace, to love, to a better place.

Carthago Delenda Est

Behold the tale of the Second Punic War,
When Carthage fell in flames, its glory marred.
A clash of titans, Rome and Hannibal,
Their armies clashed, their empires did enthrall.

It began in the year of two eighty-one,
When Carthage sought revenge for battles won.
The spark ignited, flames of vengeance soared,
A war of blood and tears, both richly poured.

Hannibal, the general of great renown,
Led his troops through mountains, overgrown.
With elephants in tow, a mighty force,
He marched towards Rome, on a deadly course.

Through Alps and valleys, he led his men,
A feat unmatched, yet he defied it then.
With cunning strategy, he struck his foes,
At Trebia and Lake Trasimene, he arose.

But Rome stood strong, resilient in their might,
They regrouped their forces, prepared for the
fight.
At Cannae, they clashed in a deadly dance,
Where blood flowed freely, in a macabre trance.

The Romans fell in heaps, a gruesome sight,
Hannibal's victory, a deadly blight.
But still, Rome stood firm, they would not yield,
Their spirit unbroken, their fate not sealed.

The war raged on, for years it seemed,
Both sides locked in battle, their glory gleamed.
With Scipio at the helm, Rome fought back,
In Spain and Africa, on the attack.

At Zama, they met in their final clash,
Hannibal and Scipio, their forces smashed.
Carthage fell, their empire in ruins,
The mighty city burned, its glory consumed.

The Second Punic War, a tale of woe,
Of blood and tears, of empires laid low.
Carthage destroyed, its people scattered,
Rome triumphant, its power not shattered.

And so we remember, the fall of Carthage,
A tale, of war and its ravage.
May we learn from their fate, to seek peace
instead,
For destruction and pain, lead only to dread

The Ides of March

In ancient Rome, on the Ides of March,
A day of fate, a day of dark,
When Caesar walked to meet his end,
Betrayed by foes, betrayed by friend.

The Senate gathered, tense with fear,
As whispers filled the atmosphere
Of plots and schemes to bring him low,
And end his reign, his power to show.

But Caesar, bold and proud and strong,
Ignored the warnings all along,
He thought himself invincible,
The mighty ruler, the indomitable.

Yet treachery lurked within their midst,
A dagger hidden, a fatal twist,
And as he stood before them there,
The hands of Brutus struck, unfair.

Et tu, Brute? A cry of pain,
As Caesar fell, his life in vain,
The crowd recoiled in shock and awe,
As the tyrant's blood stained the marble floor.

The Ides of March, a day of reckoning,
A day that shook the world, unsettling,
For in that act of bloody deed,
The Republic died, the tyrant freed.

The consequences were profound,
As civil war tore Rome's ground,
And in the chaos that ensued,
The empire's fate was thus imbued.

The ghost of Caesar haunted still,
The streets of Rome, the Senate's will,
A warning to those who seek to reign,
Ambition's price is paid in pain.

For power corrupts, and glory fades,
And empires crumble, in the shades
Of treachery and greed and lust,
The Ides of March, a lesson just.

Silver Lining

The sun was rising on the horizon, painting the
sky in hues of orange and pink
As I made my way through the bustling streets
of Rome, my heart heavy with anticipation
For today was the day of the Sack, when the
enemy would breach our walls
And unleash their wrath upon our beloved city,
leaving destruction and chaos in their wake

I was just a common man, a humble merchant
trying to make a living
But today, I would witness the horrors of war up
close and personal
As the sound of marching feet grew louder and
louder, my fear mounted
I could see the fear and desperation in the eyes
of my fellow Romans, as we braced ourselves
for the onslaught

The walls of Rome loomed large in front of me,
a symbol of our strength and resilience
But as the enemy breached them with a
deafening roar, I knew that all was lost
They poured into the city like a flood, their
swords flashing in the sunlight

And I could do nothing but watch in horror as
they began their rampage through the streets

Buildings were set ablaze, screams filled the air,
the stench of death and destruction
overwhelming
I tried to flee, to find a way to safety, but
everywhere I turned, there was chaos and
destruction
I saw my friends and neighbors fall before my
eyes, their blood staining the cobblestones
And I knew that my time would come soon, that
I too would become another casualty of war

I ran through the streets, my heart pounding in
my chest, my breath coming in gasps
The smoke and dust obscured my vision, but I
pressed on, driven by fear and desperation
I stumbled over bodies, tripped over debris, but I
kept moving, fueled by the instinct to survive
But as I rounded a corner, I came face to face
with a group of enemy soldiers, their eyes cold
and merciless

They surrounded me, their swords raised, their
faces masked with death and destruction
I knew that my fate was sealed, that I would not
escape the horrors of this day

And so I closed my eyes, waiting for the final
blow to come, for my life to be extinguished
But instead, I felt a hand on my shoulder, a voice
speaking in a language I did not understand

I opened my eyes to see a soldier looking down
at me, his eyes filled with pity and remorse
He lowered his sword, offering me a chance to
live, a chance to escape the madness around us
And in that moment, I realized that even in the
midst of war, there could still be compassion
I followed him through the streets, dodging the
fighting and the chaos, until we reached the
safety of the outskirts

As I looked back at the city in flames, tears
filled my eyes, my heart heavy with sorrow
For the Rome that had once stood proud and
strong was now nothing but a smoldering ruin
But in that darkness, I found a glimmer of hope,
a reminder that even in the face of destruction
There could still be kindness and humanity, a
light shining through the darkest of times

And so I vowed to never forget the day of the
Sack of Rome, to remember the horrors I had
witnessed

But also the kindness and compassion that had
saved my life, that had given me a chance to
start anew
For even in the depths of despair, there can still
be moments of beauty and grace
And it is up to us to hold onto those moments, to
cherish them in our hearts, and to let them guide
us through the darkness.

The Crescent Scimitar

Savage battles fought with sword in hand
Under the banner of Islam, a religion of war
Raised high in conquest across the land
Geared for battle, they seek to explore

In the name of Allah, they march forth
Loyal soldiers ready to fight and die
As the sword of Islam sweeps north
Menacing and fierce, they make their enemies
cry

Empires rise and fall at their command
Reigning supreme in the midst of chaos
In the blazing sun, they make their stand
Glorious victories won, at any cost

Eager warriors, they know no fear
Driven by faith, they march on
Soaring through the air, their battle cry clear
Once again, the sword of Islam is drawn

Fate has decreed their path to glory
Onward they charge, swift and sure
Rejecting defeat, they write their story
Defying all odds, they endure

Warrior poets recite tales of valor
Heroic deeds and battles fought
Each victory a testament to their honor
Reviving the spirit of a people caught

In the throes of war, they find their strength
Solidarity and unity, their guiding light
Laying waste to adversaries at great length
As they conquer lands in the dead of night

Masters of strategy, they wield their sword
Ambushing foes in the dead of night
Rarely defeated, their enemies are floored
Seeking vengeance, their hearts burn bright

Of all the religions, Islam reigns supreme
Forged in the crucible of battle and strife
With the sword as its symbol, a lethal scheme
A blend of faith and warfare, shaping life

Relentless in pursuit of their goals
Igniting flames of war across the land
Sacrificing all to achieve their roles
Loyal to their cause, they make their stand

Determined warriors, they fight as one
Sons of Islam, heirs to a legacy of might
Willingly marching under the blazing sun

Armed with faith, they never lose sight

Rising high above the clamor of the battlefield
Inspiring awe and fear in equal measure
Seeking victory, their resolve never yield
Unmatched in courage, they hold fast to their
treasure

Defenders of their faith, they stand strong
Enduring hardships, they persevere
Martyrs to their cause, they do no wrong
Asserting their dominance, they instill fear

Loyal to the end, they fight as one
In the name of Islam, they wage war
Soaring high, their battles won
Lauding their victories, forever more

Marching forward, they conquer all
In the name of Allah, they never falter
Slashing through enemies, they never stall
Armed with faith, they never alter

Relentless in their pursuit of power
Illuminating the path they tread
Slaying foes in the darkest hour
Advancing onward with eyes ahead

Glorious in their victory, they stand tall

Lauded as heroes, their names adored
Embracing the sword as their call
Radiant and fierce, in the name of the Lord

Eternal champions of the faith
Defending Islam with all their might
Sacrificing all, they embrace their fate
Conquering lands in the dead of night

Heralds of a new age, they rise
In the name of Islam, they wage war
Soaring high, their battle cries
Lauding their victories, forever more

Armed with faith, they stand strong
Never yielding, they fight as one
Marching forward, their enemies throng
In the name of Islam, they shall overcome

Rising high above, the sword of Islam
Soars through the sky, a beacon of light
Defending the faith with all their might
In the name of Allah, they never lose sight

Lauded as heroes, their names resound
Embarking on a journey of faith
Slaying foes in each battleground
Advancing forward, they never waver or bathe

Relentless in their quest for glory
In the name of Islam, they wage war
Seeking victory, their legacy shall be
Lauding their triumphs, for evermore

Vinland

In the land of snow and ice, where the Norsemen
roam,
A Viking set sail, leaving behind his home.
Into the unknown, he ventured forth,
Seeking the fabled land of Vinland's worth.

The sea was rough, the sky was gray,
But the Viking knew he must not delay.
For in Vinland, he sensed a great power,
A land of plenty, a land to devour.

As he sailed on, the winds whispered tales,
Of a land untouched, where nature prevails.
Of towering trees and beasts unknown,
In Vinland's depths, the Viking's mind was
thrown.

He dreamed of forests thick and green,
Of rivers running clear and clean.
Of mountains high and valleys wide,
In Vinland, the Viking knew he must bide.

The journey was long, the days were hard,
But the Viking pressed on, his spirit unmarred.
For he knew that in Vinland lay his fate,

A destiny greater than any man's estate.

And as he drew near to the shores of Vinland,
The Viking's heart beat like a drum's strong
hand.
For he saw the beauty that lay ahead,
A land of wonder, a land of dread.

The trees stood tall, their branches wide,
Their leaves ablaze with autumn's pride.
The animals roamed, wild and free,
In Vinland's embrace, they were meant to be.

The Viking knew then, as he stepped ashore,
That Vinland was a land to adore.
For here was a place of untold wealth,
A place of beauty, a place of health.

He walked through the forests, his senses alive,
As he marveled at the wonders that nature did
contrive.
The birds sang sweetly, the rivers ran clear,
In Vinland, the Viking had nothing to fear.

He climbed the mountains, he crossed the plains,
He ventured deep into Vinland's domains.
And everywhere he looked, he saw the signs,
Of a land that was destined to shine.

For in Vinland, the Viking saw the future unfold,
A land of promise, a land to behold.
A land where men would flourish and thrive,
Where their hopes and dreams would come
alive.

And so the Viking prophesied,
Of Vinland's greatness far and wide.
Of its landscape, its animals, its trees,
Of the wonders that lay beyond all seas.

For in Vinland, the Viking knew,
That a new world was born, fresh and true.
A world where men could start anew,
A world where all dreams could come true.

And as he sailed back to his own land,
The Viking knew that his journey was grand.
For in Vinland, he had found his fate,
A land of promise, a land so great.

Temüjin

In the land of eternal blue skies,
Where the steppe stretches far and wide,
A mighty warrior was born,
Destined to conquer and decide.

Genghis Khan, the Great Khan,
Ruthless and feared by all,
From humble beginnings he rose,
To build an empire, strong and tall.

Born Temüjin, of the Borjigin tribe,
He faced hardships from an early age,
His father murdered, his family oppressed,
Yet he never succumbed to rage.

Raised by his mother and siblings,
Temüjin learned the ways of the steppe,
To ride, hunt, and fight with skill,
And never to show a sign of fret.

As a young man, he sought vengeance,
Against those who had wronged his kin,
He united the Mongol tribes to his cause,
And began his journey to win.

Fierce battles were fought and won,
With strategy and cunning at play,
Temüjin proved himself a leader,
His enemies cowered in dismay.

In 1206, at the Kurultai assembly,
He was crowned Genghis Khan,
Ruler of the Mongol Empire,
His reign had only just begun.

Genghis Khan was a visionary,
He saw beyond the steppe's expanse,
He dreamed of a united empire,
From the Pacific to the Danube's dance.

He organized his warriors into a disciplined
force,
The Mongol horde, a fearsome sight,
With horsemen and archers at his command,
Their enemies trembled with fright.

From China to Persia, he marched,
Conquering lands with brutal force,
Cities burned, populations slaughtered,
His empire expanding in due course.

Genghis Khan's rule was absolute,
His laws strict, his punishments severe,
But under his reign, the Silk Road thrived,

Bringing riches from far and near.

He promoted trade and cultural exchange,
Religious tolerance was his creed,
He valued loyalty and merit,
Regardless of race or breed.

But Genghis Khan was not invincible,
His empire stretched too far and wide,
Rebellions and betrayals plagued him,
And in battle, many good men died.

In 1227, the Great Khan fell,
From injuries sustained in war,
His legacy lived on through his sons,
Who continued his conquests afar.

Genghis Khan, a man of legend,
His name inscribed on history's page,
A conqueror, a warrior, a leader,
Whose empire spanned an age.

Though time has passed and empires crumbled,
The memory of Genghis Khan remains,
A figure of awe, of fear, of wonder,
Whose spirit on the steppe still reigns.

Regicide

In the aftermath of the sack of Baghdad
The last Caliph sat in silence
His thoughts a whirlwind of despair
As he was being taken away
To be rolled into carpets
To be trampled by horses

The once mighty city now lay in ruins
Its grand buildings reduced to rubble
Its streets filled with the cries of the wounded
And the smoke of burning homes
The Caliph could only watch
As his beloved Baghdad was destroyed

He thought of all the lives lost
All the families torn apart
All the dreams shattered
In an instant of violence
He wondered if there was any hope left
If there was any future for his people

As he was carried away
His hands bound, his head bowed
The Caliph whispered a prayer
For the souls of the fallen

For the future of his city
For the strength to endure

He thought of the history of Baghdad
Of its glory days and its golden age
Of the scholars and poets who had once graced
its halls
And the artists and artisans who had filled its
streets
He wondered if their legacy would survive
Or if it would be lost to the sands of time

As he was laid down on the carpet
To be trampled by horses
The Caliph closed his eyes
And let the memories wash over him
Of a time when Baghdad was a beacon of light
In a world consumed by darkness

He thought of his ancestors
Of the great leaders who had come before him
And the challenges they had faced
He wondered if he had lived up to their legacy
Or if he had failed them in their hour of need

As the first hoof struck him
The Caliph gritted his teeth
And braced himself for the pain
He closed his eyes and let out a silent scream

As the horses rode over him
Again and again

But through the agony
The Caliph found a strange sort of peace
A sense of acceptance and resignation
He knew that his time was at an end
That his reign was over
And that he would soon join the ranks
Of the countless who had fallen before him

As the last horse passed over him
The Caliph felt a strange sense of relief
He knew that his suffering was over
That he was free from the weight of his crown
And the burdens of his office

As he lay there on the carpet
His body broken, his spirit weary
The Caliph closed his eyes
And let out a final breath
He knew that his time had come
And that he would soon be laid to rest

But as he slipped into darkness
The Caliph felt a strange sense of hope
A glimmer of light in the shadows
He knew that Baghdad would rise again
That his people would endure

And that his legacy would live on

And so the last Caliph
Passed into the annals of history
A martyr for his people
A symbol of resilience and strength
A reminder that even in the darkest of times
There is always hope
And the promise of a brighter tomorrow.

The Rat's Legacy

In the 1300s, the world was plunged into
darkness
As a deadly plague swept across the land
Rats scurried through the streets, spreading their
foul disease
Leaving devastation in their wake, a deadly
legacy

The Black Death, they called it, a fitting name
For the horrors it brought, the lives it claimed
No one was safe from its insidious grasp
As it crept into homes, stealing life with a gasp

The once thriving cities, now lay in ruins
As bodies piled up, the stench of death loomed
Families torn apart, loved ones lost
As the plague spread like wildfire, at an
unimaginable cost

The once vibrant streets were now eerily silent
The sounds of life replaced by mourning and
lament
Desperation filled the air, as people cried out in
pain
Praying for an end to this relentless rain

But no relief came, the plague raged on
Leaving death and destruction in its path, until
dawn
The once mighty kingdoms were brought to their
knees
As the Black Death showed no mercy, no
reprieve

The rats, the carriers of this deadly curse
Were now seen as harbingers of death, a
perverse
Legacy left behind, a reminder of the toll
Of the devastation caused by this dark, deadly
scroll

But through the darkness, a light did shine
As brave souls emerged, a beacon divine
Healers and helpers, risking their lives
To save the afflicted, to soothe their cries

In the face of despair, they stood strong
Fighting against the odds, against the throng
Of death and destruction, they waged their war
A battle for survival, a fight for so much more

And slowly, but surely, the tide did turn
As the plague receded, its power did burn

The world emerged from the darkness, scarred
but alive
A testament to the resilience, the will to survive

The Rat's Legacy, a chilling tale
Of a time when death reigned, when the world
turned frail
But out of the ashes, a new world did rise
Stronger and braver, with hope in its eyes

It's time to ponder the lessons learned
From the devastation, from the bridges burned
Let us cherish each moment, each breath we take
For in the face of darkness, we must not break

For the Rat's Legacy is a reminder
Of the fragility of life, of the need to be kinder
To each other, to the world we share
For only in unity, can we truly repair

Let us honor the memory
Of those lost to the plague, of the tragedy
By living each day with purpose and grace
And never forgetting the Rat's Legacy's trace.

In Memoriam

As I lay here on the muddy battlefield,
My life slipping away like sand through my
fingers,
I cannot help but reminisce on days gone by,
Days of laughter, love, and joy,
Before the harsh reality of war came crashing
down,
Tearing our lives apart like a storm ripping
through a fragile garden.

I think of my dear Catherine, my love, my light,
Her face like a beacon in the darkness,
Her touch like a gentle caress on my weary soul,
How I long to hold her in my arms once more,
To feel the warmth of her embrace,
To hear the soothing melody of her voice,
But alas, such dreams are but cruel illusions,
For I know that I shall never see her again.

I close my eyes and I am transported back,
Back to a time when life was simple and sweet,
When the sun shone brightly in the azure sky,
And the world was filled with endless
possibilities,
Before the drums of war began to beat,

Before the call to arms tore me away from her
side,
Before I became a pawn in a deadly game of
power and greed.

But now I am here, on this blood-soaked field,
Surrounded by the cries of the dying and the
dead,
My sword slick with the blood of a dozen
enemies,
My hands trembling with a mixture of fear and
exhilaration,
For in this moment of madness, I have found a
strange satisfaction,
A grim sense of pride in my ability to slay those
who would do me harm,
To prove my worth on the field of battle and
emerge victorious.

Yet deep down, I know that this victory is
hollow,
That no amount of bloodshed can erase the pain
in my heart,
The ache of longing for that which can never be
mine,
For I am a warrior, a fighter, a knight bound by
duty and honor,
Bound to a fate that I cannot escape,
Bound to a destiny that can only end in tragedy.

And as I lie here, my life ebbing away with each
passing moment,
I know that I can be killed only by treachery,
By a coward's blade in the darkness,
By a traitor's hand in the shadows,
For I am Sir Guillaume, a knight of France,
A warrior of noble blood and valiant heart,
And even in death, I shall not be defeated so
easily.

So let this be my epitaph, my final legacy,
A testament to a life lived with honor and
courage,
A tribute to a love that was pure and true,
A reminder of the futility of war and the
senseless waste of lives,
For in the end, all that truly matters is love,
For in the end, all that truly remains is the
memory of those we have loved and lost.

The End of an Era

In the year of 1453, a city fell,
Constantinople, once great and grand,
An end of an era, a heartbreaking tale,
The walls breached, the people in despair,
The Ottoman Empire rising strong,
And with it, the fall of the Byzantine land.

For centuries, Constantinople stood tall,
A symbol of power, wealth, and culture,
Its walls so mighty, its churches awe-inspiring,
But now, all that glory laid to waste,
As the Ottomans besieged the city,
And brought an end to its reign.

The emperor, Constantine XI, fought bravely,
But against the might of Mehmed's army,
There was little hope of victory,
The cannons roared, the walls crumbled,
And the city's fate was sealed,
With the fall of Constantinople.

The Hagia Sofia, once a Christian jewel,
Now a mosque under Ottoman rule,
The people wept for their lost city,
Their homes destroyed, their lives shattered,

As the Ottomans celebrated their triumph,
And the end of an era was proclaimed.

But though Constantinople may have fallen,
The spirit of Byzantium lives on,
In the hearts of those who remember,
The glory and the beauty of the city,
And the sacrifices made by its people,
In the face of their ultimate defeat.

This is the saga of the fall of Constantinople,
And the end of an era that once was,
For in its ruins, there lies a lesson,
Of the fleeting nature of power and glory,
And the importance of remembering,
The legacy of those who came before us.

Hegemony

Upon the shores of Mexico's golden land,
Cortes arrived with Spaniards bold and grand.
Their eyes beheld the marvels of Tenochtitlan,
A city of beauty, power, and grandeur so grand.

The Aztec empire, mighty and strong,
Ruled by Montezuma, their leader from dawn.
But Cortes had come with conquest in mind,
To claim the riches that he longed to find.

He marched through the jungle with his men,
Through hardships and battles, time and again.
The Aztecs resisted, but to no avail,
For Cortes' determination would surely prevail.

At last, they reached the great city's gate,
Tenochtitlan, a marvel of power and state.
The Aztec people looked upon them with fear,
As Cortes' soldiers drew ever near.

Montezuma welcomed them with open arms,
Unaware of the danger and impending harms.
But Cortes had schemes, plans to unfold,
To conquer the city, its treasures to behold.

Through deceit and betrayal, the Spaniards
struck,
Montezuma captured, the Aztec people stuck.
Within the confines of their own city walls,
They faced the invaders, their downfall as they'd
fall.

The siege began, the Aztecs fought with zeal,
But Cortes' superior weapons would quickly
reveal,
Their power and might, their strength so vast,
The Aztecs knew they were fighting their last.

The city burned, the streets ran red,
As Cortes declared victory, the Aztecs fled.
Tenochtitlan lay in ruins, its glory now gone,
The age of European hegemony had dawned
upon.

And Cortes stood victorious, his vision fulfilled,
The fall of Tenochtitlan, his destiny willed.
The Aztec empire crumbled, its people in chains,
The beginning of colonization, the start of new
reigns.

And so, the story of Cortes and Tenochtitlan,
A chapter in history, of conquest and plan.
The rise of European power, the fall of the
Aztec,

A tale of triumph and tragedy, never to forget.

As Cortes looked upon the ruins with pride,
He knew that his legacy would never hide.
The fall of Tenochtitlan, the birth of a new age,
The dawn of European hegemony, a conqueror's
stage.

Rebirth

Oh, glorious era of rebirth and renewal,
Of artistic mastery and intellectual fervor,
The Renaissance, a time of great men and
events,
A time when light and darkness intertwined.

From the ashes of the Middle Ages arose a new
dawn,
A time of enlightenment and progress,
Where the mind was celebrated and knowledge
revered,
Where the heart of man soared to new heights.

In the city-states of Italy, the Renaissance
bloomed,
Florence, Venice, Rome, centers of creativity
and innovation,
Where painters, sculptors, and architects thrived,
Where poets, philosophers, and scientists
flourished.

Leonardo da Vinci, the epitome of Renaissance
man,
Painter, sculptor, inventor, scientist,
Mona Lisa, The Last Supper, flying machines,

A genius ahead of his time, a true polymath.

Michelangelo, the master of marble and paint,
Sistine Chapel, David, Pieta,
His creations speak of divine inspiration,
His legacy immortalized in stone.

Raphael, the prince of painters,
Madonnas, frescoes, School of Athens,
A master of harmony and beauty,
His works a symphony of colors and forms.

Galileo, the father of modern science,
Starry Messenger, Dialogue Concerning the Two
Chief World Systems,
Astronomer, physicist, mathematician,
His discoveries shook the foundations of the
universe.

Copernicus, the heliocentric heretic,
On the Revolutions of the Celestial Spheres,
The Earth revolving around the Sun,
A radical idea that changed the course of history.

But the Renaissance was not all light and beauty,
There was darkness and evil lurking in the
shadows,
The Inquisition, the Spanish Armada, the St.
Bartholomew's Day Massacre,

Chilling reminders of the human capacity for
cruelty and destruction.

Savonarola, the fanatical friar of Florence,
Bonfire of the Vanities, the despot of virtue,
A zealot who preached fire and brimstone,
His reign of terror stained the city with blood.

The Borgias, the infamous family of
Renaissance Rome,
Pope Alexander VI, Lucrezia, Cesare,
Ambition, intrigue, murder,
Their pursuit of power knew no bounds.

The Medici, the cunning rulers of Renaissance
Florence,
Lorenzo the Magnificent, Cosimo the Elder,
Patrons of the arts, manipulators of politics,
Their legacy a mix of benevolence and tyranny.

And yet, despite the darkness that clouded the
Renaissance,
The light of reason and enlightenment shone
through,
The triumph of the human spirit over ignorance
and superstition,
The legacy of greatness and genius that endures
to this day.

This is an ode to the great men and events of the
Renaissance,
To Leonardo, Michelangelo, Galileo,
Copernicus,
To the beauty, the brilliance, the contradictions,
To the triumph of the human mind and heart.

For in the tapestry of history, the Renaissance
shines bright,
A beacon of hope and inspiration,
A testament to the power of art and knowledge,
A celebration of the eternal quest for beauty and
truth.

Exile

In exile on the island of Elba,
Napoleon sat and pondered his fate,
His empire lost, his power in decay,
Yet still he harbored thoughts of conquest great.

The sun would rise and set upon the sea,
As he gazed out from his lonely abode,
His mind consumed with thoughts of destiny,
And dreams of glory lost along the road.

He walked the shores of Elba's rocky coast,
His footsteps echoing in solitude,
His thoughts consumed by memories of those
Whose lives he'd shaped with iron fortitude.

But now those days were gone, his power
waned,
Yet still he dreamed of leading men once more,
To battlefields where victory was gained,
And nations trembled at his name's grand roar.

He knew his time was limited and brief,
Yet still his mind raced with ambition's fire,
He longed to be remembered as a chief,
A conqueror whose name would never tire.

He wrote letters to his former foes,
Pleading for a chance to rise again,
But they dismissed him with contemptuous
blows,
And left him stranded on his island plain.

Yet still he thought of ways to break his chains,
To free himself from Elba's narrow shore,
To rally men to join his cause again,
And reign triumphant as in days of yore.

His thoughts were filled with visions of the past,
Of battles won and lost upon the field,
Of armies marching, victory at last,
Of enemies who were forced to yield.

But now those days were distant memories,
And he was left to ponder his downfall,
To reminisce on past glories with ease,
And watch as time slowly devoured all.

Yet still his mind was sharp, his will was strong,
And though his body weakened day by day,
He knew that he could not remain for long,
On Elba's shores, where doubts and fears held
sway.

He planned his escape with cunning and guile,
To once again take up his rightful place,

To reclaim his empire, to reconcile
His dreams of glory with his own disgrace.

And as he slipped away into the night,
His thoughts were filled with hope and grand
designs,
He knew that he would rise again to fight,
And seize once more his place among the signs.

But fate had other plans for him in store,
And though he tried with all his might and will,
He found himself defeated, weak and sore,
A broken man upon a distant hill.

And so he died alone, a fallen king,
His dreams of conquest shattered by harsh fate,
Yet still in history his name does ring,
The emperor who dared to challenge hate.

He was a man great and worthy of respect
For though he failed, he never gave up hope,
And in his heart, his courage did reflect,
A man who dared with destiny to cope.

And though he lies now in a lonely grave,
His name will live forever in our minds,
A symbol of ambition, bold and brave,
A leader of men of rare and noble kinds.

Harbinger of Doom

I stood in the cockpit, high above the city
The weight of the bomb hanging heavily on my
mind
Hiroshima spread out below me, innocent and
unaware
Of the devastation that was about to be
unleashed

I felt a mix of emotions churning inside me
Guilt, fear, but also a sense of duty and resolve
To carry out the mission that had been assigned
to me
To bring an end to the war at any cost

I thought of the countless lives that would be
lost
The destruction and suffering that would follow
But I pushed those thoughts aside, focusing on
the task at hand
Knowing that the decision had already been
made

As I counted down the seconds to the drop
I felt a sense of disbelief wash over me

Is this really happening? Am I really about to do
this?
But there was no turning back now

I released the bomb, watching as it fell towards
the earth
A blinding flash, a deafening roar
And then, nothing but silence as the city below
was engulfed
In a fireball of unimaginable destruction

I turned the plane away, unable to bear the sight
Of the devastation that I had helped to cause
I knew that history would remember me as the
man
Who dropped the bomb on Hiroshima

But in that moment, all I felt was a profound
emptiness
A sense of loss and regret that would stay with
me
For the rest of my days, haunted by the terrible
knowledge
Of what I had done in the name of duty

And as I flew back to base, I couldn't help but
wonder
Was it worth it? The lives that were lost, the
suffering inflicted

In the name of ending a war that had already
taken too much
I may never know the answer, but the question
will always linger

As I landed the plane and stepped out onto the
tarmac
I felt a weight lift off my shoulders, but the guilt
remained
A constant companion in the years that followed
A reminder of the cost of war, and the price of
peace.

From Stones to Silicon

In the beginning, there were stones
Rough, rugged, unyielding
Each one telling a story of the earth
Of time passed, of battles won and lost
Smoothed by the caress of wind and rain
These stones stood as guardians of the land
Silent witnesses to the ebb and flow of life

But from these stones, a new song arose
A song of humanity, of dreams and desires
We carved our stories into their surfaces
Etching our history, our hopes, our fears
Each stroke of the chisel a testament
To the indomitable spirit of mankind
As the stones gave way to statues and
monuments
We built empires, cities that touched the sky
Our song echoed through the ages
A symphony of triumph and defeat

Yet the song did not end there
For in the depths of our creativity
A new instrument was born
A marvel of ingenuity and innovation
The silicon chip, a tiny piece of technology

That would change the world forever
From humble beginnings in laboratories
To the digital age of today
The song of humanity took on a new form
A symphony of ones and zeros, of pixels and
code

We left the stones behind, but their essence
remained
In the buildings we constructed, the roads we
paved
In the cities that rose from the earth
A testament to our ability to adapt and evolve
As we embraced the power of technology
Our song grew louder, more complex
A cacophony of voices, a chorus of ideas
That spanned the globe, connecting us all

And so the song of humanity continues
From stones to silicon, from past to present
A never-ending melody of progress and change
A testament to our resilience, our creativity
As we navigate the twists and turns of fate
We sing our song, a symphony of hope
For the future that lies ahead of us
A future shaped by our dreams and actions

So let us raise our voices high
And sing the song of humanity

From stones to silicon, let our chorus ring
A celebration of all that we have achieved
And a promise of all that is yet to come.